Romain Rolland   Samuel Taylor Coleridge

Paul Jakob Deussen   Linda McCartney

oreau   Martin Luther

bald Wheeler   Mark Twai

halil Gibran   Saadi   David

r. Arnold Toynbee   Benjamin Franklin

handas Gandhi   Omar Khayyam

Bradley Miller   Oliver Goldsmith

ocrates   Thomas Moffett   Aurobindo

William C. Roberts   Ella Wheeler Wilcox

n Cowper   Matthew Arnold

eterlinck   Prophet Mohammed   Seneca

n   Berke Breathed   Cesar Chavez   Hu Shih

offler   Victor Hugo   Thomas Edison

A. Parthasarathy   Josh Billings

sky   Ludwig von Schroder   Robert Burns

dous Huxley   Robert Browning

penhauer   Edward Wallis Hoch

ylvain Bailly   K.D. Lang   Richard Wagner

Gogh   Oliver Wendell Holmes

helley   Plutarch   Richard Chenevix Trench

Edward Carpenter   Leibnitz

Victor Cousin   William Wordsworth

W. Longfellow   Isaac Bashevis Singer

Karl Wilhelm Friedrich Schlegel

orge Robert Stowe Mead   Apollonius Tyaneus

CITATIONS
TRIBUTES QUOTES

Compiled by
A. Parthasarathy

First Edition 2019

ISBN No: 978-93-81094-34-1

Published by:
A. Parthasarathy
1A Landsend
Mumbai 400 006
India
www.vedantaworld.org

Printed by:
Parksons Graphics Pvt. Ltd.
Taloja Industrial Area
Navi Mumbai 410 208
India

CONTENTS

PREFACE

This work presents a selection of interesting facts about India, tributes to Vedanta, philosophic, spiritual and literary quotes and certain observations on vegetarianism.

These citations should inspire readers to pursue, investigate the fundamental realities of life and living. A preparation for the present and the future of human existence.

A. Parthasarathy

CHAPTER I

FACTS REGARDING INDIA

India conquered and dominated
China culturally for 20 centuries
without ever having to send a single
soldier across her border.
Hu Shih, Ambassador of China to USA
(1891 - 1962)

I like to think that someone will trace
how the deepest thinking of India
made its way to Greece and from there
to the philosophy of our times.
John Archibald Wheeler, Physicist (b.1911)

7

If there is a country on earth which can justly claim the honour of having been the cradle of the Human race or at least the scene of primitive civilization, the successive developments of which carried into all parts of the ancient world and even beyond, the blessings of knowledge which is the second life of man, that country is assuredly India.

The Encyclopaedia Britannica

In India I found a race of mortals living upon the earth, but not adhering to it. Inhabiting cities, but not being fixed to them, possessing everything but possessed by nothing.

Apollonius Tyaneus, Greek Thinker
(1st Century AD)

The history of India for many centuries had been happier, less fierce, and more dreamlike than any other history. In these favourable conditions, they built a character - meditative and

peaceful and a nation of philosophers
such as could nowhere have existed
except in India.
H.G. Wells, Sociologist, Historian, Author
(1866-1946)

It will no longer remain to be doub-
ted that the priests of Egypt and the
sages of Greece have drawn direct-
ly from the original well of India,
that it is to the banks of the Ganges
and the Indus that our hearts feel
drawn as (if) by some hidden urge.
Friedrich Mejer Jean-Sylvain Bailly,
French Astronomer (1736-1793)

If there is one place on the face of
earth where all the dreams of living
men have found a home from the very
earliest days when man began the
dream of existence, it is India!
Romain Rolland, French Scholar

The motion of the stars calculated

by the Hindus before some 4500 years vary not even a single minute from the tables of Cassine and Meyer (used in the 19th century). The Hindu systems of astronomy are by far the oldest --- the Egyptians, Greeks, Romans and even the Jews derived from the Hindus their knowledge.

Jean-Sylvain Bailly, French Astronomer
(1736-1793)

She (India) has left indelible imprints on one fourth of the human race in the course of a long succession of centuries. She has the right to reclaim ... her place amongst the great nations sum- marizing and symbolizing the spirit of humanity. From Persia to the Chinese sea, from the icy regions of Siberia to Islands of Java and Borneo, India has propagated her beliefs, her tales, and her civilization!

Sylvia Levi, French Scholar

To other countries, I may go as a tourist,
but to India, I come as a pilgrim.
Martin Luther King, Jr.

India is the cradle of the human race,
the birthplace of human speech, the
mother of history, the grandmother of
legend, and the great grandmother of
tradition. Our most valuable and most
instructive materials in the history of
man are treasured up in India only!
Mark Twain (1835-1910)

Nothing has been left undone, either
by man or nature, to make India the
most extraordinary country that the
sun visits on his rounds.
Mark Twain

In religion, India is the only millionaire
... The One land that all men desire
to see and having seen once, by even
a glimpse, would not give up that
glimpse for all the shows of all the

11

rest of the globe combined.
Mark Twain

If I were asked under what sky the human mind has most fully developed some of its choicest gifts, has most deeply pondered on the greatest problems of life, and has found solutions, I should point to India.
Max Mueller

If I am asked which nation had been advanced in the ancient world in respect of education and culture then I would say it was - India.
Max Mueller, German Indologist

India was the mother of our race and Sanskrit the mother of Europe's languages. She was the mother of our philosophy, mother through the Arabs, of much of our mathematics, mother through Buddha, of the ideals embodied in Christianity, mother

through village communities of
self-government and democracy.
Mother India is in many ways the
mother of us all.
          Will Durant

Many of the advances in the sciences
that we consider today to have been
made in Europe were in fact made
in India centuries ago.
Grant Duff, British Historian of India

We owe a lot to the Indians, who
taught us how to count, without
which no worthwhile Scientific
discovery could have been made.
          Albert Einstein

It is already becoming clearer that
a chapter which has a western beginning will have to have an Indian
ending if it is not to end in the self-
destruction of the human race ---
At this supremely dangerous moment

in history the only way of salvation
for mankind is the Indian way.
Dr. Arnold Toynbee, British Historian
(1889-1975)

Nearly all the philosophical and
mathematical doctrines attributed
to Pythagoras are derived from India.
Ludwig von Schroder

Not until we see the richness of the
Hindu mind and its essential spiri-
tuality can we understand India.
Lyn Yutang, Chinese prolific Writer
(1895-1976)

India never invaded any country
in her last 10000 years of history.

India has the world's third largest
active army, after China and USA.

India has been the largest troop
contributor to the United Nations

Peacekeeping Missions since its inception.

When many cultures were only nomadic forest dwellers over 5000 years ago, Indians established Harappan culture in Sindhu Valley. (Indus Valley Civilisation)

The name 'India' is derived from the River Indus, the valleys around which were the home of the early settlers. The Aryan worshippers referred to the river Indus as the Sindhu. India's name is derived from the 'Indus' river. Indus Valley Civilisation is the world's oldest civilisation. India, hence, is the world's oldest, most advanced and continuous civilisation.

The Persian invaders converted it into Hindu. The name 'Hindustan' combines Sindhu and Hindu and thus refers to the land of the Hindus.

Chess was invented in India.

Algebra, Trigonometry and Calculus are studies, which originated in India.

The 'Place Value System' and the 'Decimal System' were developed in India in 100 B.C.

Buttons were invented in India. Yes, your shirt buttons.

We also invented the ruler. And shampoo. And discovered the number zero. And the value of pi. And cataract surgery. And plastic surgery. And diamond mining. And water on the moon.

The World's First Granite Temple is the Brihadeswara Temple at Tanjavur, Tamil Nadu. The shikhara of the temple is made from a single 80-tonne piece of granite. This magnificent temple was built in just five years, (between 1004 AD and 1009 A.D) during the reign of Rajaraja Chola.

India is the largest democracy in the world, the 7th largest Country in the world, and one of the most ancient civilizations.

The game of Snakes and Ladders was created by the 13th century poet saint Gyandev. It was originally called 'Mokshapat'. The ladders in the game represented virtues and the snakes indicated vices. The game was played with cowrie shells and dices. In time, the game underwent several modifications, but its meaning remained the same, i.e. good deeds take people to heaven and evil to a cycle of re-births.

The world's first university was established in Takshila in 700 B.C. More

than 10,500 students from all over
the world studied more than 60 subjects.
The University of Nalanda built in the
4th century was one of the greatest
achievements of ancient India in the
field of education.

Ayurveda is the earliest school of medicine known to mankind. The Father
of Medicine, Charaka, consolidated
Ayurveda 2500 years ago.

India was one of the richest countries till the time of British rule in
the early 17th Century. Christopher Co-
lumbus, attracted by India's wealth,
had come looking for a sea route to
India when he discovered America by mistake.

The Art of Navigation & Navigating
was born in the river Sindh over 6000
years ago. The very word Navigation
is derived from the Sanskrit word
NAVGATIH. The word navy is also

derived from the Sanskrit word Nou.

Bhaskaracharya rightly calculated the time taken by the earth to
orbit the Sun hundreds of years before the astronomer Smart. Accor-
ding to his calculation, the time taken
by the Earth to orbit the Sun was
365·258756484 days.

The value of 'pi' was first calculated
by the Indian Mathematician Budha-
yana, and he explained the concept
of what is known as the Pythagorean
Theorem. He discovered this in the
6th century, long before the European
mathematicians.

Algebra, Trigonometry and Calculus
also originated in India. Quadratic
Equations were used by Sridhara-
charya in the 11th century. The largest
numbers the Greeks and the Romans
used were 106 whereas Hindus used

numbers as big as 10*53 (10 to the power of 53) with specific names as early as 5000 B.C. during the Vedic period. Even today, the largest used number is Terra: 10*12 (10 to the power of 12).

Until 1896, India was the only source of diamonds in the world.
(Source: Gemological Institute of America)

The Baily Bridge is the highest bridge in the world. It is located in the Ladakh valley between the Dras and Suru rivers in the Himalayan mountains. It was built by the Indian Army in August 1982.

Usage of anaesthesia was well known in ancient Indian medicine. Detailed knowledge of anatomy, embryology, digestion, metabolism, physiology, etiology, genetics and immunity is also found in many ancient Indian texts.

India exports software to 90 countries.

The four religions born in India – Hinduism, Buddhism, Jainism and Sikhism are followed by 25% of the world's population.

Jainism and Buddhism were founded in India in 600 B.C. and 500 B.C. respectively.

Islam is India's and the world's second largest religion.

There are 300,000 active mosques in India, more than in any other country, including the Muslim world. And the third largest Muslim population in the world.

The oldest European church and

synagogue in India are in the city of Cochin. They were built in 1503 and 1568 respectively.

Jews and Christians have lived continuously in India since 200 B.C. and 52 A.D. respectively.

The largest religious building in the world is Angkor Wat, a Hindu Temple in Cambodia built at the end of the 11ᵗʰ century.

The Vishnu Temple in the city of Tirupathi built in the 10ᵗʰ century, is the world's largest religious pilgrimage destination. Larger than either Rome or Mecca, an average of 30,000 visitors donate USD 6 million to the temple everyday.

Sikhism originated in the Holy city of Amritsar in Punjab. Famous for housing the Golden Temple, the city was founded in 1577.

Two major religions, Buddhism and Jainism, were established in India.

Varanasi, also known as Benares, was called 'the Ancient City' when Lord Buddha visited it in 500 B.C. and is the oldest, continuously inhabited city in the world today.

India provides safety for more than 300,000 refugees originally from Sri Lanka, Tibet, Bhutan, Afghanistan and Bangladesh, who escaped to flee religious and political persecution.

Martial Arts were first created in India and later spread to Asia by Buddhist missionaries.

Yoga has its origins in India and has existed for over 5000 years.

India has the second largest English speaking population in the world.

And despite budgetary constraints, India's space program is one of the top 5 space programs in the world.

The first country to consume sugar. India was the first country to develop extraction and purifying techniques of sugar. Many visitors from abroad learnt the refining and cultivation of sugar from India.

India has the largest numbers of vegetarians in the world. So much so that Pizza Hut had to open their first pure vegetarian restaurant in the country. And KFC had to introduce a 'vegetarian' menu for India. And so did McDonalds, the world's largest fast-food manufacturer.

Today, India is the world's third largest economy.

India is one of only three countries that makes supercomputers (the US and Japan are the other two).

The world's second largest road network is in India – over 4·86 million kilometers of roads cover the country.

India's tech capital, Bangalore, has increased its office supply by six times since 2006, and now has more Grade-A offices than Singapore.

India is the largest producer of films in the world.

The world's highest cricket ground is in Chail, Himachal Pradesh. Built in 1893 after leveling a hilltop, this cricket pitch is 2444 meters above sea level.

India has the largest number of Post Offices in the world.

The largest employer in India is the Indian Railways, employing over a million people.

The human calculator, Shakuntla Devi was given this title after she demonstrated the calculation of two 13 digit numbers: 7,686,369,774,870 × 2,465,099,745,779 which were picked at random. She answered correctly within 28 seconds.

Rabindranath Tagore is credited not only for writing the Indian national anthem but the Bangladeshi national anthem as well. He was also offered knighthood by the British but refused the honour after the Jalianwala Bagh massacre.

CHAPTER II

TRIBUTES TO VEDANTA

Eminent theologists regard Vedanta of the Upanishads as a world scripture. A scripture appealing to pursuers of Truth in all races at all times without distinction. Some of their observations below bear testimony to it.

Arthur Schopenhauer 1788-1860. A great German philosopher. His philosophy is unmistakably transfixed with the doctrines expounded in the Upanishads.

On Vedanta he says: In the whole world there is no study so beneficial and so elevating as that of the Upanishads. It has been the solace of my life, it will be the solace of my death.

Max Müller 1823-1900. A renowned German orientalist. Comments on this assertion of Schopenhauer: If the words of such an independent philosopher require any endorsement, with my lifelong study of all the religions in the world and all the systems of philosophy in Europe, I humbly endorse this experience of Schopenhauer. If philosophy or religion is meant to be preparation for the afterlife, a happy life and happy death, I know of no better preparation for it than Vedanta.

Paul Jakob Deussen 1845-1919. A Sanskrit scholar of the University of Kiel, Germany: I find the philosophy of

Parmenides, Plato and Kant in a nutshell in Vedanta and advise the Indians - Vedanta in its unfalsified form, is the strongest support of pure morality, is the greatest consolation on the sufferings of life and death. Indians, keep to it.

Karl Wilhelm Friedrich Schlegel 1772-1829. A German poet-philosopher: The highest stretches of European philosophy appear as dwarfish pigmies before the grand, majestic Titan of Upanishadic thought. It cannot be denied that the early Indian possessed the knowledge of the true God, all their writings are replete with sentiments and expressions, noble, clear and severally grand, as deeply concerned and reverentially expressed as in any human language in which men have spoken of their God. And the divine origin of man is continually circulated to stimulate his efforts to return, to animate him in the struggle and incite him to consider a re-union and re-corporation with Divinity as the one primary object of every action and exertion.

John Gough 1757-1825. An English philosopher: The Upanishads are the loftiest utterances of Indian intelligence.

Sir William Jones 1746-1794. An English scholar and Supreme Court judge: The Greeks derived their knowledge from Vedanta, the clear, comprehensive system of philosophy of the Hindus of India.

Victor Cousin 1792-1867. Historian and philosopher of France: There can be no denying that the ancient Hindus possessed the knowledge of the true God. Their philosophy, their thought is so sublime, so elevating, so accurate and true that any comparison with the writings of the Europeans appears like a Promethean fire stolen from heaven as in the presence of the full glow of the noonday sun.

George Robert Stowe Mead 1863-1933. An English author and theosophist eulogises: The Upanishads are a world scripture. Written thousands of years ago by the wise Indian seers - simple and graceful in inspiring Sanskrit poetry. A matchless record of Brahmavidya, the knowledge of Brahman, the supreme God.

Henry David Thoreau, American Philosopher 1817-1862. Whenever I have read any part of the Vedas, I have felt that some unearthly and unknown light illuminated me. In the great teaching of the Vedas, there is no touch of the sectarianism. It is of ages, climes and nationalities and is the royal road for the attainment of the Great Knowledge. When I am at it, I feel that I am under the spangled heavens of a summer night.

Further insights from Indian sages.

Sri Aurobindo 1872-1950. Indian Seer and poet: The Upanishads are a kind of poetry – word of vision and rhythm of the Spirit – that has not been written before or after. Alone of extant scriptures gives one and all without veil of stinting, with plenitude and a noble catholicity the truth of the supreme God, Brahman. Its aid to humanity is therefore indispensable.

Swami Vivekananda 1863-1902. Renowned spiritual Leader: While every other religion depended on the life of its founder, Vedanta was based upon eternal principles. It was on this that it based its claim of being the universal religion. All ideals are true and the different religious systems were but special paths for the attainment of these various ideals, which when intensified, were certain to draw out the divinity in man.

Swami Rama Tirtha 1873-1906. The greatest Apostle of Truth pronounces: Vedanta brings you a religion which is found in the streets, which is written upon the leaves, which is murmured in the brooks, which is whispered in the winds, which is throbbing in your veins and arteries, a religion which concerns your business and bosom, a religion which you have not to practise by going to a particular church, mosque or temple only, a religion which you have to practise and live in your everyday life about your hearth, in your dining room, everywhere.

These are some of the glorious tributes paid by savants and sages to the Upanishads, Vedanta. The Upanishads remain the highest authority in all matters pertaining to philosophy and religion besides being the earliest extant literary monuments of India.

CHAPTER III

PHILOSOPHIC QUOTES

All grumbling is tantamount to
"Oh! Why is the lily not an oak?"

ANON

As you think so you become, is a
law of life.

ANON

He gave, he forgave.

ANON

I had no shoes and complained until

I met a man who had no feet.
Saadi

A person thinking rationally today is a needle in a haystack.
A. Parthasarathy

Your motto in Life should be :
To strive, to struggle, not to succeed.
Anon

Life is an arrow shot from darkness, flutters in the light for a while and vanishes back into darkness.
Matthew Arnold

The trouble with most folks is not so much their ignorance, as their knowing so many things which ain't so.
Josh Billings

Never before could I have believed it but I see it all now. There is no

happiness unless you have clean
dropped thinking about yourself;
but you must not do it by halves.
While even there is a least grain of
self left, it will spoil it all. You must
just leave it all behind and vouch-
safe the personality and mind
that much sympathy as to any
stranger, no more, no less.
                    Edward Carpenter

A pessimist sees the difficulty in
every opportunity; an optimist sees
the opportunity in every difficulty.
                    Winston Churchill

Never let your present happiness
Lean on your future acquisition.
                    A. Parthasarathy

Setting an example is not the main
means of influencing others, it is the
only means.
                    Albert Einstein

We cannot solve our problems with the same thinking that brought us these problems.

Albert Einstein

Transform your unilateral passion into universal adoration.

A. Parthasarathy

I do not feel obliged to believe that the same God who has endowed us with sense, reason and intellect has intended us to forego their use.

Galileo Galilei

Marriage is like a temple resting on two pillars. If they come too close to each other the temple will collapse.

Khalil Gibran

And there are those who give and know not pain in giving, nor do they seek joy, nor give with mind-

fulness of virtue; they give as in
yonder valley the myrtle breathes
its fragrance into space.
                    Khalil Gibran

Faith is a belief in a thing I do not
know until I come to know what I
believe in.
                    Joel Goldsmith

The darkest hour of Life is when you
plan to get money without earning it.
                    Horace Greely

It is not the world that distresses
you but how you relate to it. It is
not whom or what you meet in life
that matters but how you meet it.
                    A. Parthasarathy

For him in vain the envious seasons
roll who bears eternal summer in his
soul.
                    Oliver Wendell Holmes

Life is to give, not to take.
                    Victor Hugo

In our discussion of social evolution
we must remember that the very
perfection of society must always
appear as imperfection, for a highly
developed society is dynamic. A static
society is in a condition of arrested
development. The most highly developed organism shows the greatest
imperfections.
                    David Starr Jordan

Work can never tire you. What tires
you is your worry over the past and
anxiety for the future.
                    A. Parthasarathy

You may at times need to use your
temper but never lose your temper.
                    A. Parthasarathy

There is just one way to bring up
a child in the way he should go

and that is to travel that way yourself.
          Abraham Lincoln

Happy and blessed hour, when wic-
kedness stands forth revealed as
goodness bereft of its guide.
          Maurice Maeterlinck

The wise talk because they have
something to say. Fools talk because they have to say something.
                    Plato

When something can be read without effort, great effort has gone
into its writing.
          Enrique Jardiel Poncela

Gratitude is not only the greatest
of virtues, but the parent of all others.
          Cicero (54 B.C.)

The more things are forbidden,
the more popular they become.
          Mark Twain

Your home should be the centre, not the boundary of your affection.

A. Parthasarathy

It is difficult to find happiness in oneself but it is impossible to find it anywhere else.

Arthur Schopenhauer

The acquisition of riches has been to many not an end to their miseries, but a change in them. The fault is not in the riches, but the disposition.

Seneca

To suffer from a disease is bad enough. And not being aware of it could prove fatal. People are totally blind to the epidemic of attachment.

A. Parthasarathy

When I passed a shop I was amazed
at the number of things man can
do without.

Socrates

If I were as big a reader as others,
I should have been as big an ignoramus
as others.

Herbert Spencer

Living is an art, skill, technique.
You need to learn and practise it.
As you would to play a musical
instrument or fly an aircraft.

A. Parthasarathy

Intellectual growth should commence
at birth and cease only at death.

Albert Einstein

Your mind plays havoc. Use your
intellect to overpower it.

A. Parthasarathy

Every man is a divinity in disguise,
a god playing the fool.

Ralph Waldo Emerson

Intellect is invisible to the man who
has none.

Arthur Schopenhauer

Your likes and dislikes are not to
be suppressed, stifled or strangled.
Your intellect has only to examine
and deal with them appropriately
to ensure your life runs smooth. A
human can ill afford to let the whim
and fancy of the mind take over
his personality.

A. Parthasarathy

Iron and gold are good for buying
iron and gold and that is all.

Swami Rama Tirtha

Intense work is rest.

Swami Rama Tirtha

The perfection of wisdom and the end of true philosophy is to proportion our wants to our possessions, our ambitions to our capacities, we will then be a happy and a virtuous people.

Mark Twain

The way to gain anything is to lose it.

Swami Rama Tirtha

Faith is a bird that feels the light and sings while the dawn is still dark.

Rabindranath Tagore

The world is full of sound scholars but not sound men.

Rabindranath Tagore

The illiterate of the 21st century will not be those who cannot read and write but those who cannot learn, unlearn and relearn.

Alvin Toffler

A stone that is fit for the wall is not left in the way.

Richard Chenevix Trench

Your spouse & you ride on your children's back crushing them with your load. And yet assure yourselves and others that you are sorry for them and wish to lighten their burden by all means possible except by getting off their back.

A. Parthasarathy

A banker is a fellow who lends you his umbrella when the sun is shining, but wants it back the minute it begins to rain.

Mark Twain

Whenever you find yourself on the side of the majority, it is time to pause and reflect.

Mark Twain

So many gods, so many creeds, so
many paths that wind & wind, while
just the art of being kind is all the
sad world needs.

Ella Wheeler Wilcox

To expect adverse happenings is
being a pessimist, to be prepared
for them is a philosopher.

A. Parthasarathy

Only two things are infinite, the
universe and human stupidity,
and I'm not sure about the former.

Albert Einstein

Westerner or easterner, educated
or uneducated, prince or pauper
— everyone, everywhere suffer from
the devastating virus of attachment.
And graver still humans pass this
virus on to the lives of their descendants.

A. Parthasarathy

I have never let my schooling inter-
fere with my education.
                    Mark Twain

Reading without reflecting is like
eating without digesting.
                    Edmund Burke (1729-1797)

Relationships built on rights shall
perish and those built on duties
flourish.
                    A. Parthasarathy

It ain't what you don't know that
gets you into trouble. It's what you
know for sure that just ain't so.
                    Mark Twain

Golf is a good walk spoiled.
                    Mark Twain

Golf is a day spent in a round of
strenuous idleness.
                    William Wordsworth

When I was young and free and my imagination had no limits, I dreamed of changing the world. As I grew older and wiser, I discovered the world would not change, so I shortened my sights somewhat and decided to change only my country.

But it, too, seemed immovable. As I grew into my twilight years, in one last desperate attempt, I settled for changing only my family, those closest to me, but alas, they would have none of it.

And now as I lie on my death bed, I suddenly realize: If I had only changed myself first, then by example I would have changed my family. From their inspiration and encouragement, I would then have been able to better my country and, who knows, I may have even changed the world.

Quote inscribed on tomb of

an Anglican Bishop buried in the crypt of Westminster Abbey.

To escape plague the only way is to live up to the law of hygiene.
                                    Anon

There is so much good in the worst of us, and so much bad in the best of us, that it hardly behooves any of us to talk about the rest of us.
                        Edward Wallis Hoch

They talked about and about, I came out of the same door I entered.
                        Omar Khayyam

Life sleeps in plants, dreams in animals and wakes in man.
                                Leibnitz

The wise learn from the experience of others, fools from their own.
                        Romanian Proverb

Fools rush in where angels fear to tread.

Alexander Pope

It is not enough to be industrious; so are the ants. What are you industrious about?

Henry David Thoreau

By all means get married, if you get a good wife you will be happy, if you get a bad one you will become a philosopher!

Socrates

It grieves my heart to think what man has made of man, when every flower enjoys the air it breathes.

William Wordsworth

The beauty and grandeur of human activity is renunciation IN action, not renunciation OF action.

A. Parthasarathy

CHAPTER IV

SPIRITUAL QUOTES

Do not believe what you have heard.
Do not believe in tradition because
it is handed down many generations.
Do not believe in anything that has
been spoken of many times.
Do not believe because the written
statements come from some old sage.
Do not believe in conjecture.
Do not believe in authority or teachers
or elders.
But after careful observation and
analysis, when it agrees with reason

and it will benefit one and all, then
accept it and live by it.
                    Lord Buddha

Ask and it shall be given to you;
knock, and it shall be opened unto you.
                    Jesus Christ

Blessed are the pure in heart, for they
shall see God.
                    Jesus Christ

Iniquity there shall be in this world;
woe unto you if you be the cause.
                    Jesus Christ

Judge not others; resist not evil.
                    Jesus Christ

Get thee behind me Satan, I will
have none at thy hands.
                    Jesus Christ

Father, forgive them, they know not

what they do.
> Jesus Christ

He that findeth his life shall lose it:
And he that loseth his life for my
sake shall find it.
> Jesus Christ

May you enjoy bliss through renunciation.
> Ishavasya Upanishad

He who does not realise the Self here
in his lifetime suffers immeasurable
loss.
> Kena Upanishad

That supreme Reality, Brahman is
your Self within and not what you
worship here in the world.
> Kena Upanishad

He is best among human beings
who is best at repaying.
> Prophet Mohammed

Laa ilaha illallah: There exists nothing but God.

Prophet Mohammed

Whatsoever the superior person does that alone other people do, whatever standard he sets that the world follows.

Bhagavad Gita

He who eats without producing is verily a thief.

Bhagavad Gita

You must raise yourself by yourself.

Bhagavad Gita

To those who are attuned to the Self with constant and unswerving focus, spiritual progress and enlightenment is assured.

Bhagavad Gita

True happiness is like poison in the beginning but nectar in the end. False happiness is like nectar in the beginning but poison in the end.

Bhagavad Gita

The Bhagavad Gita is one of the clearest and most comprehensive summaries of the perennial philosophy ever to have been done. Hence its enduring value, not only for the Indians, but also for all mankind. It is perhaps the most systematic spiritual statement of the perennial philosophy.

Aldous Huxley (1894-1963)

Self is God ...   Upanishads

I am that I am...   Old Testament

The kingdom of God is within you.
---   New Testament

The greatest jihad is that for the conquest of Self... 'Quran

I am the Self in all beings... Gita

FROM A. PARTHASARATHY

If you do not find peace in action, you will never find it.

A spirit of service and sacrifice to the society is the mark of civilisation.

Meditation is the art of the intellect holding the mind on a single thought to the exclusion of all other thoughts.

A perfect human being is one who has emotion and is not emotional; has passion and not passionate; has sentiment, not sentimental.

Prayer and worship has been reduced to licensed beggary.

The fall of the human intellect has
caused an explosion of the mind
leaving behind a holocaust of attachment - threatening extinction of the
human race.

You make yourself, you mar yourself.
You are the architect of your fortune,
the architect of your misfortune.

You get what you deserve, not what
you desire.

True renunciation is that capacity
in you to set the right value for all
that the world offers, to consider
them ephemeral and inconsequen-
tial even while you may be amidst
them, perhaps enjoying them.

Just reflect: Does light come from the
moon? Delight from the world?

Religion has personified desire as the devil standing between human and God.

Christianity : Satan
Islam : Shaitan
Buddhism : Mara
Hinduism : Asura

You are to give up not your worldly possessions but your attitude of possessiveness towards them. Not persons but your infatuation for them.

Name, fame, power, position, status, money, family are the toys that make your joys.

CHAPTER $\overline{V}$

LITERARY QUOTES

Perhaps, the most valuable result of all education is the ability to make yourself do the thing you have to do when it ought to be done, whether you like it or not. It is the first lesson that ought to be learned and however early a person's training begins, it is probably the last lesson a person learns thoroughly.

Thomas Huxley

The mind is its own place, and in itself can make a heaven of hell, a hell of heaven.

John Milton

Liberal education, viewed in itself is simply the cultivation of the intellect, as such, and its object is nothing more or less than that of intellectual excellence.

Cardinal Newman

Intelligence is acquired through external agencies, from schools and universities while the intellect is developed by oneself. By observing two disciplines:

1. Never accept anything for granted
2. Question everything

A. Parthasarathy

Forgiveness is the fragrance the violet releases as the foot crushes it.

Mark Twain

Stuck to their Web-site, inter-Net
or Cell-phone. Caught up in a web,
net or cell all through life, yet people claim to be free!

A. Parthasarathy

He who cannot reason is a fool; he
who will not is a bigot; he who
dare not is a slave.

William Drummond

The most intelligent person he
had ever met in his life is his
tailor! When he was asked why he
thought so, he promptly answered,
"Because he is the only one who takes
fresh measurements every time I
go to him."

George Bernard Shaw

That low man seeks a little thing
to do, Sees it and does it;
This high man, with a great thing
to pursue, Dies ere he knows it.

That low man goes on adding one
to one, His hundred's soon hit;
This high man, aiming at a million,
Misses a unit.
                Robert Browning

The best laid schemes of mice and
men gang aft agley.
                Robert Burns

The tsunami of greed has swallowed
up giant corporations and companies
causing financial crashes round the
world.
                A. Parthasarathy

I am monarch of all I survey;
My right there is none to dispute.
                William Cowper

People who live in glass houses
should not throw stones.
                Geoffrey Chaucer (1385)

The nakedness of the indigent world
may be clothed from the trimmings
of the vain.
                Oliver Goldsmith

And what is friendship but a name.
A charm that lulls to sleep;
A shade that follows wealth or fame,
But leaves the wretch to weep?

And love is still an emptier sound
The modern fair one's jest:
On earth unseen, Or only found
To warm the turtle's nest.
                Oliver Goldsmith

Character is to have power and not
use it.
                A. Parthasarathy

Ere you remark another's sin,
Bid thy own conscience look within.
Control thy more voracious bill,
Nor for a breakfast nations kill.
                John Gay

Our dear delights are often such,
Expos'd to view but not to touch;
The sight our foolish heart inflames,
We long for pineapples in frames,
With hopeless wish one looks and lingers,
One breaks the glass and cuts his fingers,
But they whom truth and wisdom lead,
Can gather honey from a weed.
>> William Cowper

To bring about sanity in this world
change TGIF into TGIM.
>> A. Parthasarathy

A group of people, occupying a
geographical place, over a long period of time, respecting certain values
of life, develop a fragrance of their
own. That fragrance is their culture.
>> A. Parthasarathy

To them his heart, his love, his
>> griefs were given,

But all his serious thoughts had
            rest in Heaven.
As some tall cliff that lifts its
                awful form,
Swells from the vale, and midway
            leaves the storm,
Though round its breast the rolling
            clouds are spread,
Eternal sunshine settles on its head.
            Oliver Goldsmith

And, as a bird each fond endearment
                tries
To tempt its new-fledged offspring
            to the skies,
He tried each art, reproved each
            dull delay,
Allured to brighter worlds and led
            the way.
            Oliver Goldsmith

Fame is sought by an intoxicated
ego.
            A. Parthasarathy

It is a far, far better thing I do, than
I have ever done;
It is a far, far better rest that I go
to than I have ever known.
Charles Dickens

He prayeth well who loveth well
both man and bird and beast.
He prayeth best who loveth best
all things both great and small.
Samuel Coleridge

Time management
= Work management
= Self management
A. Parthasarathy

Where wealth accumulates, men
decay.
Oliver Goldsmith

Give your personality a lift, you
lift the whole world.
A. Parthasarathy

From William Shakespeare

All the world's a stage
And all the men and women merely
players;
They have their exits and their
entrances.
As You Like It

Costly thy habit as thy purse can
buy,
But not express'd in fancy; rich,
not gaudy.
Hamlet

Give every man thine ear,
But few thy voice.
Hamlet

I am cruel only to be kind.
Hamlet

Ingratitude stronger than
traitors' arms,
Quite vanquished him.
Julius Caesar

O, beware of jealousy; it is the
green-eyed monster;
which doth mock the meat it feeds
on.
                    Othello

O thou invisible spirit of wine,
If thou hast no name to be known
by, let us call thee devil !
                    Othello

Reputation is an idle and most
                    false imposition;
Oft got without merit and lost
                    without deserving.
                    Othello

Who steals my purse steals trash.
                    Othello

She is of so free, so kind, so apt,
so blessed a disposition that she holds
it a vice in her goodness not
to do more than she is requested.
                    Othello

This above all : To thine own self be true,
And it must follow, as the night the day,
Thou canst not then be false to any man.
Hamlet

When remedies are past, the griefs
are ended
By seeing the worst, which late on
hope depended.
Othello

CHAPTER $\overline{VI}$

ON VEGETARIANISM

Animals are my friends... and I don't eat my friends.

George Bernard Shaw

How can you eat anything with eyes?

Will Kellogg

Nothing will benefit human health and increase chances for survival of life on Earth as much as the evolution to a vegetarian diet.

Albert Einstein

If slaughterhouses had glass walls, everyone would be a vegetarian. We feel better about ourselves and better about the animals, knowing we're not contributing to their pain.

Paul McCartney

For as long as men massacre animals, they will kill each other. Indeed, he who sows the seed of murder and pain cannot reap joy and love.

Pythagoras (6th century BC)

A man can live and be healthy without killing animals for food; therefore, if he eats meat, he participates in taking animal life merely for the sake of his appetite. And to act so is immoral.

Leo Tolstoy

Humans destroy animals or birds or fishes for the sake of their palate. Food has no taste before it reaches the tongue. Nor after it leaves the tongue. Yet, for the few seconds' pleasure they do not hesitate to slaughter millions upon millions of innocent creatures, day after day.

A. Parthasarathy

As long as there are slaughterhouses, there will be battlefields.

Leo Tolstoy

We all love animals. Why do we call some "pets" and others "dinner?"

K.D. Lang

Dear Lord, I've been asked, nay commanded, to thank Thee for the Christmas turkey before us ... a turkey which was no doubt a lively, intelligent bird ... a social being ... capable of actual affection ... nuzzling its young with almost human-like compassion. Anyway, it's dead and we're gonna eat it. Please give our respects to its family.

Berke Breathed

Among the noblest in the land —
Though man may count himself the least — That man I honour and revere, who without favour, without fear, in the great city dares to stand, the friend of every friendless beast.

Henry W. Longfellow

While we ourselves are the living graves of murdered beasts, how can we expect any ideal conditions on this earth?

George Bernard Shaw

Coexistence ... What the farmer does with the turkey — until Thanksgiving.

Mike Connolly

A mind of the calibre of mine cannot

derive its nutriment from cows.

George Bernard Shaw

It is strange to hear people talk
of Humanitarianism, who are mem-
bers of societies for the prevention
of cruelty to children and animals,
and who claim to be God-loving men
and women, but who, nevertheless,
encourage by their patronage the
killing of animals merely to gratify
the cravings of appetite.

Otoman Zar-Adusht Ha'nish

You put a baby in a crib with an
apple and a rabbit. If it eats the
rabbit and plays with the apple,
I'll buy you a new car.

Harvey Diamond

Flesh eating is simply immoral,
as it involves the performance of
an act, which is contrary to moral
feeling: killing. By killing, man

suppresses in himself, unnecessarily, the highest spiritual capacity, that of sympathy and pity towards living creatures like himself and by violating his own feelings becomes cruel.

Leo Tolstoy

I have from an early age abjured the use of meat, and the time will come when men such as I will look upon the murder of animals as they now look upon the murder of men.

Leonardo da Vinci

To my mind, the life of a lamb is no less precious than that of a human being. I should be unwilling to take the life of a lamb for the sake of the human body.

Mohandas Gandhi

Flesh eating is unprovoked murder.
Benjamin Franklin

We stopped eating meat many years ago. During the course of a Sunday lunch we happened to look out of the kitchen window at our young lambs playing happily in the fields. Glancing down at our plates, we suddenly realized that we were eating the leg of an animal who had until recently been playing in a field herself. We looked at each other and said, "Wait a minute, we love these sheep -- they're such gentle creatures. So why are we eating them?" It was the last time we ever did.
Linda and Paul McCartney

My dream is that people will come to view eating an animal as cannibalism.
Henry Spira

In every respect, vegans appear to enjoy equal or better health in comparison to both vegetarians and non-vegetarians.

T. Colin Campbell, Cornell University

There will come a time ... when civilised people will look back in horror on our generation and the ones that preceded it: the idea that we should eat other living things running around on four legs, that we should raise them just for the purpose of killing them! The people of the future will say "meat-eaters!" in disgust and regard us in the same way we regard cannibals and cannibalism.

Dennis Weaver

The animals you eat are not those who devour others; you do not eat the carnivorous beasts, you take them as your pattern. You only hunger after sweet and gentle creatures who harm no one, which follow you, serve you, and are devoured by you as the reward of their service.

John Jacques Rousseau

When we kill the animals to eat them, they end up killing us because their flesh, which contains cholesterol and saturated fat, was never intended for human beings.

William C. Roberts, M.D.

If man wants freedom why keep birds and animals in cages? Truly man is the king of beasts, for his brutality exceeds them. We live by the death of others. We are burial places!

Leonardo da Vinci

Not to hurt our humble brethren is our first duty to them, but to stop there is not enough.

St. Francis of Assisi

Men dig their graves with their own teeth and die by those fated instruments more than the weapons of their enemies.

Thomas Moffett

You have just dined, and however scrupulously the slaughter house is concealed in the graceful distance of miles, there is complicity.

Ralph Waldo Emerson

There is no fundamental difference between man and the higher animals in their mental faculties --- the lower animals, like man, manifestly feel pleasure and pain, happiness and misery.

Charles Darwin

If experiments on animals were abandoned on grounds of compassion, mankind would have made a fundamental advance.

Richard Wagner

It were much better that a sentient being should never have existed, than that it should have existed only to endure unmitigated misery.

Percy Bysshe Shelley

What I think about vivisection is that if people admit that they have the right to take or endanger the life of living beings for the benefit of many, there will be no limit for their cruelty.

Leo Tolstoy

When it comes to having a central nervous system, and the ability to feel pain, hunger and thirst, a rat is a pig is a dog is a boy.

Ingrid Newkirk

I have no doubt that it is part of the destiny of the human race in its gradual improvement to leave off eating animals.

Henry David Thoreau

Until he extends the circle of compassion to all living things, man will not himself find peace.

Dr. Albert Schweitzer

If you have men who will exclude any of god's creatures from the shelter of compassion and pity, you will have men who will deal likewise with their fellowmen.

St. Francis of Assisi

Basically we should stop doing those things that are destructive to the environment, other creatures and ourselves and figure out new ways of existing.

Moby

It is just like man's vanity and impertinence to call an animal dumb because it is dumb to his dull perceptions.

Mark Twain

We consume the carcasses of creatures of like appetites, passions and organs of our own, and fill the slaughterhouses daily with screams of pain and fear.

Robert Louis Stevenson

To a man whose mind is free there is something even more intolerable in the sufferings of animals than in the suffering of man. For with the latter it is at least admitted that suffering is evil and that the man who causes it is a criminal. But billions of animals are mercilessly butchered everyday without a shadow of remorse. If any man were to refer to it, he would be thought ridiculous. And that is the unpardonable crime.

Romain Rolland - Nobel 1915

Non-violence leads to the highest
ethics, which is the goal of all evolution.
Until we stop harming all other living
beings, we are still savages.

Thomas Edison

To become vegetarian is to step into
the stream which leads to Nirvana.

Buddha

Since visiting the abattoirs of S. France
I have stopped eating meat.

Vincent Van Gogh

I feel very deeply about vegetarianism
and the animal kingdom. It was my
dog Boycott who led me to question
the right of humans to eat other sentient beings.

Cesar Chavez

Love animals: God has given them the rudiments of thought and joy untroubled. Do not trouble their joy, don't harass them, don't deprive them of their happiness, don't work against God's intent. Man, do not pride yourself on superiority to animals; they are without sin, and you, with your greatness, defile the earth by your appearance on it, and leave the traces of your foulness after you – alas, it is true of almost every one of us!

Fyodor Dostoyevsky

The worst sin towards our fellow creatures is not to hate them, but to be indifferent to them, that's the essence of inhumanity.

Isaac Bashevis Singer

It is man's sympathy with all creatures that first makes him truly a man.

Dr. Albert Schweitzer-Nobel 1952

A vegetarian is a person who won't
eat anything that can have children.
David Brenner

Teaching a child not to step on a caterpillar is as valuable to the child,
as it is to the caterpillar.
Bradley Miller

Man is the only animal that can
remain on friendly terms with the
victims he intends to eat until he
eats them.
Samuel Butler

We pray on Sundays that we may
have light
To guide our footsteps on the path
we tread;
We are sick of war, we don't want
to fight,
And yet we gorge ourselves upon
the dead.
George Bernard Shaw

If you knew how meat was made,
you'd probably lose your lunch.

K.D. Lang

A man of spiritual intensity does
not eat corpses.

George Bernard Shaw

The eating of meat extinguishes
the seed of great compassion.

Mahaparinirvana

I do feel that spiritual progress
does demand that we should cease
to kill our fellow creatures for the
satisfaction of our bodily wants.

Mohandas Gandhi

One farmer says to me, "You cannot
live on vegetable food solely, for it
furnishes nothing to make the bones with;" and so he religiously
devotes a part of his day to sup-
plying himself with the raw material

of bones; walking all the while he
talks behind his oxen, which, with
vegetable-made bones, jerk him and
his lumbering plow along in spite of
every obstacle.
Henry David Thoreau

Think of the fierce energy concentra-
ted in an acorn! You can bury it in the
ground, and it explodes into an oak!
Bury a sheep, and nothing happens
but decay.
George Bernard Shaw

My situation is a solemn one. Life is
offered to me on condition of eating
beefsteaks. But death is better than
cannibalism. My will contains direc-
tions for my funeral, which will be followed not by mourning coaches, but
by oxen, sheep, flocks of poultry, and
a small travelling aquarium of live
fish, all wearing white scarves in honour
of the man who perished rather than eat

his fellow creatures.
George Bernard Shaw

I did not become a vegetarian for my health; I did it for the health of the chickens.
Isaac Bashevis Singer

Suppose that tomorrow a group of beings from another planet were to land on Earth, beings who considered themselves as superior to you as you feel yourself to be to other animals. Would they have the right to treat you as you treat the animals you breed, keep and kill for food?
John Harris

Heart attacks... God's revenge for eating his little animal friends.
Anon.

Vegetarian food leaves a deep impression on our nature. If the whole world

adopts vegetarianism, it can change
the destiny of humankind.
                    Albert Einstein

Our task must be to free ourselves ...
widening our circle of compassion to
embrace all living creatures and the
whole of nature and its beauty.
                    Albert Einstein

The greatness of a nation and its
moral progress can be judged by
the way its animals are treated.
                    Mohandas Gandhi

If we cut up beasts simply because
they cannot prevent us and because we
are backing our own side in the struggle for existence, it is only logical to
cut up imbeciles, criminals, enemies
or capitalists for the same reasons.
                    C. S. Lewis

A human body in no way resembles

those that were born for ravenousness;
it hath no hawk's bill, no sharp talon,
no roughness of teeth, no such strength
of stomach or heat of digestion, as
can be sufficient to convert or alter
such heavy and fleshy fare. But if you
will contend that you were born to an
inclination to such food as you have
now a mind to eat, do you then yourself
kill what you would eat. But do it
yourself, without the help of a
chopping-knife, mallet or axe, as
wolves, bears and lions do, who
kill and eat at once. Rend an ox
with thy teeth, worry a hog with
thy mouth, tear a lamb or a hare
in pieces, and fall on and eat it
alive as they do. But if thou had rather
stay until what thou eat is to become dead, and if thou art loath
to force a soul out of its body, why then
dost thou against nature eat an
animate thing? There is nobody that
is willing to eat even a lifeless and

a dead thing even as it is; so they
boil it, and roast it, and alter it by
fire and medicines, as it were, changing and quenching the slaughtered gore with thousands of sweet
sauces, that the palate being there-
by deceived may admit of such un-
couth fare.

Plutarch

The assumption that animals are
without rights and the illusion
that our treatment of them has
no moral significance is a positive-
ly outrageous example of Western
crudity and barbarity. Universal compassion is the only guarantee of morality.

Arthur Schopenhauer

LIVING GRAVES

We are the living graves of murdered
beasts,
Slaughtered to satisfy our appetites.

We never pause to wonder at our
feasts,
If animals, like men, can possibly
have rights.
We pray on Sundays that we may
have light,
To guide our footsteps on the path
we tread.
We're sick of war, we do not want
to fight —
The thought of it now fills our
hearts with dread,
And yet — we gorge ourselves upon
the dead!

Like carrion crows we live and feed
on meat,
Regardless of the suffering and
the pain
we cause by doing so, if thus we
treat
defenceless animals for sport or
gain,
how can we hope in this world to

attain,
the PEACE we say we are so
anxious for.
We pray for it o'er hecatombs
of slain,
to God, while outraging the
moral law,
thus cruelty begets its offspring –
WAR.
George Bernard Shaw

PUBLICATIONS OF

A. PARTHASARATHY

The Complete Works of Swami
Parthasarathy ... 2532 pages

The Fall of the Human Intellect
... 168 pages

Governing Business & Relationships
... 216 pages

The Holocaust of Attachment
... 204 pages

Select English Poems
... 128 pages

Vedanta Treatise: The Eternities
... 436 pages

Bhaja Govindam & Atmabodha
... 232 pages

Bhagavad Gita ...1080 pages

Choice Upanishads...364 pages

Thesis on God ... 180 pages

The Symbolism of Hindu Gods
and Rituals ... 183 pages

Citations Tributes Quotes
...100 pages

www.vedantaworld.org

VEDANTA WORLD APP

The App is available on Apple App

Store and Google Play Store.

Search for 'Vedanta World'.

Download links also available

on www.vedantaworld.org/app

E-LEARNING COURSE ON VEDANTA

Complete course on Vedanta
Philosophy   ... 3 years

Guidelines on Business & Relationships
                              ... 1 year

A Direction for Youth   ... 1 year

Mould your Children   ... 1 year

elearning.vedantaworld.org

A. Parthasarathy is an internationally acclaimed philosopher with a multi-disciplined academic base including postgraduation from London University. He has researched for over seventy years on the state of human beings and focused on the pressing need to revive, rehabilitate the human intellect. His resolve has emerged into four distinct avenues of service:

Vedanta Academy

Parthasarathy founded the Vedanta Academy in January 1988. The Academy is situated in Malavli Hills, 108 kms from Mumbai, India. It offers continual three-year residential courses for students from India and abroad. The course is designed to build the intellect and instil higher values of life.

Public Discourses

His discourses on intellectual development have captivated audiences the world over for more than fifty years. And have been widely acclaimed by prestigious universities, institutions and organisations.

Corporate Seminars

Parthasarathy has been a distinguished resource of the Young Entrepreneur's Organisation (YEO), Young President's Organisation (YPO), World Economic Forum and several multinational corporations.

Writings

He has authored twelve books which present the ancient philosophical wisdom of thinkers from the East and the West. Three of the books have earned the bestselling status. The *Vedanta Treatise : The Eternities* is currently in its 17th edition.

The present book entitled *Citations Tributes Quotes* has been handwritten by A. Parthasarathy at the age of 92.